Recursive Restriction Estimation: An Alternative to Post-Stratification in Surveys of Land and Forest Cover

Raymond L. Czaplewski

United States Department of Agriculture / Forest Service

Rocky Mountain Research Station

Research Publication RMRS-RP-81

August 2010

Abstract

Numerous government surveys of natural resources use Post-Stratification to improve statistical efficiency, where strata are defined by full-coverage, remotely sensed data and geopolitical boundaries. Recursive Restriction Estimation, which may be considered a special case of the static Kalman filter, is an attractive alternative. It decomposes a complex estimation problem into simple components that are sequentially processed. Compared to Post-Stratification, it more efficiently uses remotely sensed data, both continuous and categorical. It is less constrained by sample size, which is especially important with panel surveys. It produces a conditionally unbiased covariance matrix for the vector estimate of population totals without approximations or ad hoc assumptions. This facilitates variance estimates for non-linear pseudo-estimators. A robust sequential algorithm controls numerical errors inherent with Recursive Restriction Estimator, which can otherwise cause unreliable results. Analysis of residuals can detect other anomalies.

Keywords: NFI, accuracy assessment, systematic sampling, auxiliary-variables, constraints

Author

Raymond L. Czaplewski is a Research Mathematical Statistician with the USDA Forest Service, Rocky Mountain Research Station (RMRS), in Fort Collins, CO. He is a member of the RMRS Inventory, Monitoring, and Analysis Program and the Interior West Forest Inventory and Analysis (FIA) program, with headquarters in Ogden, UT. He was an RMRS Project Leader with the national FIA program, a Program Analyst with the Bighorn National Forest, and a Wildlife Planner with the Wyoming Game and Fish Department. He received his Ph.D. from Colorado State University in quantitative range science, his M.S. degree from University of Wyoming in systems ecology, and his B.A. degree from Northwestern University in biology. His professional interests include statistical estimators for sample surveys that integrate time-series of remotely sensed observations with FIA field data.

Introduction

Strategic monitoring of forest resources requires reliable estimates of the area of land use and land cover categories over large geographic regions. Accurate coverage statistics depend on accurate classification of land conditions, which typically requires expensive field measurements. These are only feasible for a probability sample of field plots. One example is the Forest Inventory and Analysis (FIA) program conducted by the U.S. Department of Agriculture, Forest Service[1]. It is the national forest inventory of the United States. FIA monitors the status, condition, and trends in forests over the entire nation (Smith 2002). Another example is the 2001 Land Use/Crop Area frame sample Survey (LUCAS-2001)[2] of the EU15 nations[3] of the European Union (Gallego and Delincé 2010). The objectives of LUCAS include consistent monitoring of the status and change in land use and land cover, including forests.

Statistical reliability of survey statistics, such as those produced by FIA and LUCAS, is constrained by the sample size of primary sampling units (PSUs). However, auxiliary remotely sensed data can improve statistical reliability with relatively little incremental cost. For example, FIA uses multispectral optical data from spaceborne sensors to classify forest conditions across the United States (Nelson and others 2007). LUCAS-2001 uses the CORINE land cover map produced by the "Co-ordination of Information on the Environment" program of the European Environment Agency (Kleeschulte and Büttner 2006). CORINE is based on photo-interpretation of optical data from spaceborne sensors to classify small, homogeneous polygons into detailed categories of land cover and agricultural use.

Each dataset of remotely sensed pixels is a full-coverage census[4] of the entire statistical population, and, therefore, complete enumeration of these pixel data contains zero sampling error. However, reliability of remotely sensed data is constrained by misclassification errors, which are caused by the inability of inexpensive remotely sensed data to agree exactly with expensive field measurements. These misclassification errors usually yield biased areal estimates (Bauer and others 1978, Houston and Hall 1984, Hay 1988, Czaplewski 1992, Gallego 2004, Gallego and Bamps 2008). My goal is to improve the statistical efficiency of unbiased estimates from a sample survey of field plots, which has sampling error but no measurement error, using a census of biased remotely sensed statistics, which have measurement error but no sampling error.

Post-Stratification

Post-Stratification (PS) with remotely sensed data and administrative districts (e.g., counties or municipalities) is widely used in surveys of forests and other natural resources (Mandallaz 2008 p. 16). Both FIA (Scott and others 2005) and LUCAS-2001 (Gallego 2004) use full-coverage remotely sensed data[4] to define strata. FIA uses administrative districts (e.g., states, counties, and municipalities) in addition to remote sensing. Credibility of government statistics often depends, in part, upon the consistency between survey estimates and known characteristics of administrative districts (Särndal and others 1992, Knottnerus 2003, Sõstra and Traat 2009). For example, the sum of estimated areas for all land uses in a county should exactly agree with the total area of that county as proclaimed in the official record.

After sampled PSUs are selected from an unstratified systematic grid, each is assigned to one stratum or, in the case of FIA, one or more strata (McRoberts and others 2005a). An independent sample survey estimate for each stratum total is separately made with the subset of PSUs in that stratum. The total area of forest cover in a stratum is an example of one estimate, but similar estimates may be produced for tens to hundreds of other variables that are measured in the field, such as land ownership, forest type, condition class, wood volume, and tree demographics. Estimates of stratum totals for each variable are summed into estimates for the entire sampled population. The associated population variance estimate uses the PS estimator (e.g., Cochran 1977 p. 135, Särndal and others 1992 p. 266, Scott and others 2005, Gallego and Bamps 2008, Mandallaz 2008 p. 18). PS is similar to two-phase sampling (Cochran 1977 p. 327) with equal inclusion probabilities among strata. Rather than explicitly defining the structure of the population or the sampling design, the following uses PS as an estimator to improve precision with a census of auxiliary categorical variables (Zhang 2000).

Limitations Imposed by Post-Stratification

PS limits opportunities to improve statistical efficiency with remotely sensed auxiliary data in at least five ways. First, the number of strata is limited by the number of PSUs. A small sample size indirectly constrains the detail available in auxiliary information that may be used to improve statistical efficiency. For example, FIA uses geopolitical units, such as groups of municipalities or counties, as strata (McRoberts 2005b p. 5). Administrative records for the area of each geopolitical stratum do not necessarily improve estimates of land cover and land use coverages (see Van Deusen 2005 for an exception). However, such strata do impose areal control so that summaries of FIA statistics agree with the officially proclaimed area of each geopolitical unit. FIA also uses full-coverage, remotely sensed Landsat data[4] that are classified into multiple categories of forest cover (e.g., McRoberts and others 2005b, Nelson and others 2007). One purpose is to improve efficiency of areal estimates for various forest conditions. However, cross-classification of numerous geopolitical units by numerous categories of remotely sensed forest conditions multiplicatively creates numerous strata, most of which have an insufficient number of PSUs for reliable stratum estimates. This is an example of the "curse of dimensionality." As a solution, FIA collapses multiple remotely sensed categories of forest cover into two simple categories: forest and nonforest. In extreme classes, FIA must further combine small geopolitical units so that each stratum as at least $n_h = 4$ field plots (Scott and others 2005, McRoberts 2006). Seminal references recommend larger sample sizes (e.g., $20 \leq n_h$; Särndal and others 1992 pp. 251 and 267, de Gruijter and others 2006 p. 118). Collapsing strata during PS not only reduces statistical efficiency, it is also inappropriate for inference unless the stratum means are expected to be equal (Cochran 1977 p. 134, Särndal and others 1992 p. 411, Knottnerus 2003 p. 169). In a citation to Jagers (1986), Zhang (2000) observes that "post-stratified estimation that ignores the empty sample post-strata is downward biased for non-negative (study-variables)."

Second, panel designs further decrease sample size. FIA uses 5 to 10 panels of PSUs to produce annual estimates (McRoberts and others 2005a, Patterson and Reams 2005). Each panel is an interpenetrating sub-sample of FIA PSUs that uniformly cover the sampled population (Bechtold and Patterson 2005). A single panel is measured each year. Therefore, only 10 to 20 percent of the total PSUs are available to produce annual estimates with PS (Reams and others 2005b). One pragmatic solution is to combine all panels into a single estimate. This increases the effective sample size, which reduces the magnitude of the estimated variances. This is the "temporally indifferent" estimator described by McRoberts (2005). It is closely related to a moving average estimator (Patterson and Reams 2005), and it is algebraically identical to the estimator previously used by FIA for decadal periodic surveys. However, changes in the condition of PSUs accumulate between acquisition of the remotely sensed data and the most recent field measurements. Disagreement between the remotely sensed and true condition of a changed plot is not distinguishable from a classification error with remotely sensed data. Loss of statistical efficiency is rapid as agreement deteriorates (Czaplewski and Patterson 2001, 2003, Fattorini and others 2004), regardless of the cause. Therefore, PS with the temporally indifferent estimator does not take full advantage of the information available in remotely sensed data. This is especially true in dynamic landscapes, which are the domains that often have the greatest demand for current monitoring data (Smith 2002). Furthermore, it is feasible to frequently monitor major changes in land cover with spaceborne sensor data (e.g., Healey and others 2005, Sader and others 2005), and these measurements might substantially improve statistical reliability (e.g., Czaplewski 1999). However, cross-classification of annual remotely sensed data with relatively rare changes in land cover along with remotely sensed measurements of more static forest conditions produces numerous small strata with few PSUs, especially with annual panel designs. Again, PS constrains the potential for using relatively inexpensive time-series of remotely sensed data to improve statistical reliability.

Third, misleading population estimates are possible for rare attributes. This condition is more frequent whenever the sampling intensity within the stratum is weak. For example, if four PSUs sampled in a small forest stratum are truly forest, then the stratum estimate will be 100 percent forest with a variance of zero. Even though the stratum truly has some non-forest cover, the stratum estimate for non-forest area would be exactly zero with seemingly perfect accuracy (i.e., estimated sampling error of zero). This is known as a "sampling zero" in the analysis of contingency tables (Agresti 2007 p. 154) and an "empty sample post-stratum" in sampling (Zhang 2000). Furthermore, uncertainty with the variance estimate for a stratum increases as sample size decreases. These problems increase as the sample size within a stratum becomes very small (e.g., $4 \leq n_h \leq 10$).

Fourth, the 0.067-ha support region for an FIA PSU can straddle strata boundaries. A portion of a single support region can occur in one geopolitical stratum, while the remainder of the support region may occur in one or more other strata. While this maintains areal control on geopolitical variables, it does so by compromising the assumed independence of sampling errors among strata in the variance estimator for PS (Hahn and others 1995, Bechtold and Patterson 2005). FIA uses a different plot expansion factor for each portion of a PSU support region residing in a different stratum

(Scott and others 2005). While this does not necessarily bias stratum estimates, it does further bias the associated variance estimator (McRoberts 2005). Van Deusen (2005) concludes that this leads to optimistic variance estimates, meaning the population estimates are not as reliable as inferred by their variance estimates. FIA assumes this bias is small and ignorable. This assumption is supported by Breidt and Opsomer's (2008) study.

A similar challenge exists with the 90-ha LUCAS-2001 PSUs and the CORINE polygons, which have a minimum polygon size of 25 ha. However, Gallego and Bamps (2008) implement a solution that differs from FIA. They classify each and every 90-ha polygon in their study domain into one, and only one, stratum. They define four strata by creating a new polychotomous categorical variable for both sampled and non-sampled PSUs. The categorical variable is based on the proportion of annual crops within the 90-ha PSU, as approximated by the CORINE land cover map. The four categories are 0 to 10 percent, 11 to 50 percent, 51 to 80 percent, and 81 to 100 percent annual crops. This approach does satisfy certain assumptions that underlie the variance estimator for PS, namely, each PSU resides in one, and only one, stratum. Again, the unintended consequence is loss of information available in the remotely sensed data. This approach also precludes exact areal control for geopolitical entities.

Fifth, PS presents challenges in accurately estimating the variance of population totals from a systematic sample, which is used both by FIA and LUCAS-2001. The PS variance estimator is an approximation that assumes simple random sampling, not systematic sampling, to calculate approximate joint inclusion probabilities among PSUs in different strata (Särndal and others 1992 Chapter 7.10.2). The joint inclusion probabilities for a systematic sampling frame differ from those in a simple random sample (Fattorini and others 2004). Furthermore, Gallego and Bamps (2008) use Matérn's (1960) model-based variance estimator for systematic sampling. Through empirical tests with LUCAS-2001 and CORINE data, Gallego and Bamps conclude that Matérn's estimator is nearly unbiased and more accurate than the design-consistent estimator, which equals the variance estimator for simple random sampling (Fattorini and others 2004). However, Gallego and Bamps were forced to use a heuristic approximation of the variance estimator for PS. Also, Matérn's variance estimator can be affected by the unique spatial distribution of PSUs within a stratum, and the variance estimator might be dominated by relatively few PSUs that happen to be located close together in space within the same stratum.

FIA also uses systematic sampling (Reams and others 2005a) and is confronted with similar issues. However, FIA uses a design-consistent variance estimator for PS (Fattorini and others 2004), which is algebraically equivalent to the assumption of simple random sampling. This is a biased approximation to the expected variance with a systematic sampling frame (Scott and others 2005). FIA accepts this small bias because it tends to overestimate the uncertainty, and is thus considered "conservative."

In summary, PS often forces omission of valuable, remotely sensed auxiliary information. This limits opportunities for increased accuracy and statistical efficiency. Annual panel surveys and areal control on geopolitical units further exacerbate these limitations. Furthermore, there are no unbiased variance estimators for PS because they are approximations, even with simple random sampling. Systematic sampling introduces additional ad hoc approximations.

Recursive Restriction Estimator

My objective is to introduce a particular expression of the Recursive Restriction Estimator (RRE) that is an alternative to PS. RRE was introduced into the statistical literature by Knottnerus (2003). This alternative mitigates the limitations imposed by PS that are elucidated above. The RRE refers to the sequential recursive application of a Restriction Estimator (RE), in which the output from one recursion is used as input to the next recursion. The recursive structure solves a complex estimation problem by decomposing it into a sequence of simpler estimation problems.

Czaplewski (2010) views RRE as a special case of the Kalman filter, namely the "static Kalman filter" (Maybeck 1979 p. 114) or the "limiting Kalman Filter" (Chui and Chen 2009 p. 77), for a time-invariant linear stochastic system (Särndal and others 1992 p. 21). The Kalman filter was originally developed as a multivariate time-series estimator for dynamic stochastic systems (Maybeck 1979 p.114, Gregoire and Walters 1988). It improves time-series estimates of the multivariate "states of the system" (e.g., vector of parameter totals for a sampled population) with a time-series of multivariate measurements of that system (e.g., remotely sensed variables). The Kalman filter accommodates random measurement errors and partial measurements (i.e., observations of some elements of the state-vector but not other elements). The Kalman filter is not used here for time-series applications. Rather, it is used here as a multivariate composite estimator (Gregoire and Walters 1988) for more efficient estimation of the vector of population totals (i.e., the state-vector) at one point in time.

Blending sample survey terms (e.g., Särndal and others 1992, Knottnerus 2003) with Kalman filter terms (e.g., Jazwinski 1970, Maybeck 1979), the state-vector includes a partition for multiple **study-variables**[5], such as the total area of forest and agriculture in the sampled population, and a vector partition for multivariate **auxiliary-variables**, such as the area of each type of land cover classified with remotely sensed data (Knottnerus 2003 pp. 50, 356, and 385). The state-vector is equivalent to the "parameter vector" used by Sõstra and Traat (2009). The **estimated state-vector** is fully identified through a probability sample and an appropriate sample survey estimator (e.g., Hansen-Hurvitz estimator). In the case of LUCAS-2001 and FIA, the partition for the study-variables (e.g., area of forest, area of cropland, and biomass) for each sampling unit are measured in the field. The remaining partition for the auxiliary-variables is determined by precisely registering the geographic coordinates of each sampling unit to a geospatial database, such as a Geographical Information System (GIS) or a full-coverage image of Landsat pixels[4].

The **measurement vector** is an independent[6] observation of the state-vector. In the context of RRE below, the measurement vector contains, in part, the census totals for all remotely sensed auxiliary-variables. However, this directly measures only a portion of the state-vector, namely, the partition with the auxiliary-variables. RRE improves the estimated population totals for the auxiliary-variables in the state-vector. This indirectly improves estimates of the study-variables through the cross-covariance among auxiliary- and study-variables in the state-vector.

As illustrated by Czaplewski (2001) in the context of sample surveys, Householder (1964), Diderrich (1985), and Maybeck (1979 p. 213) use the matrix inversion lemma (e.g., Chui and Chen 2009 p. 3) to prove the algebraic identity among the generalized least squares estimator, the multivariate composite estimator, and the static Kalman filter. Knottnerus (2003 p. 315) uses the perspective of Pythagorean regression to make the same connection between the Kalman filter and estimators for complex sample surveys, including constraints on the estimands through the RE and the sequential estimation with the RRE. I consider RE and RRE to be synonymous with the static Kalman filter and the recursive multivariate composite estimator, which might also be viewed as special cases of pseudo-estimators (Särndal and others 1992 p. 173). Therefore, the Kalman filter is algebraically identical to estimators that are more familiar in the sample survey literature. In addition, the Kalman filter literature abounds with pragmatic solutions to numerical errors, which are stubborn obstacles to optimal estimation algorithms in the sample survey literature (Särndal and others 1992 p. 241, Estevao and Särndal 2004 p. 657). Furthermore, the static Kalman filter does not require computation of complicated joint inclusion probabilities, which can change as new field data and remotely sensed data accumulate. Other advantages of the Kalman filter appear in the "Discussion."

The next section uses a realistic case study to communicate better the motivation, conceptual approach, and mathematical details of the RRE as a more efficient alternative to PS. Implementation issues are illuminated, and related approaches to more complex estimators are briefly mentioned.

Case Study and Methods

The case study employs the example by Gallego and Bamps (2008) who use the CORINE land cover map to post-stratify LUCAS-2001 PSUs. Their goal was improved reliability of areal coverage estimates of LUCAS-2001 land use categories (Table 1). They defined an analysis domain as the 10-km buffer from the EU15[3] coastline, which covers about 10 percent of the EU15 nations. There are $m = 1114$ PSUs in the domain[7]. This design has several challenging elements, and it is well suited to illustrate the advantages of RRE relative to PS.

The 90-ha LUCAS-2001 PSU is a cluster plot that nominally contains 10 Secondary Sampling Units (SSUs). If the PSU intersects a domain boundary, it will have fewer SSUs. Each SSU is classified with the LUCAS-2001 field protocol into one of 57 categories of land cover and one of 14 categories of land use. The cluster plot may be heterogeneous, where SSUs can have different classifications in the LUCAS-2001 system. To simplify this case study as an example, the classification system is collapsed into nine broad categories of land use (Table 1).

Gallego and Bamps (2008) used a GIS to intersect the location of each LUCAS-2001 SSU with the corresponding CORINE polygon. This allowed further cross-classifications of each LUCAS-2001 SSU into one of the 44 CORINE categories of land cover. Classification protocols differ between LUCAS-2001 and CORINE. The former uses ground measurements made by field crews for the sample of 0.0009-ha (3- by 3-m) SSUs, while the latter uses remote sensing to classify polygons that are 25 ha or larger. The classification systems also differ. For example, LUCAS-2001 defines forest as patches of at least 0.5 ha exceeding 10 percent crown cover and 5 m in tree height. CORINE requires each forest patch exceed

Table 1. Cross-classification of CORINE and LUCAS-2001 categories from the non-stratified LUCAS-2001 sample of cluster plots (Gallego and Bamps 2008) and comparison to the census statistics from the CORINE land cover map (thousands of km^2).

CORINE Land Cover Categories	LUCAS Land Use Categories										Census Totals from the CORINE Land Cover Map
	Artificial surfaces	Annual crops	Temporary pastures, fallow fields	Permanent grass cover	Olive trees	Vineyards, other permanent crops	Forest	Woodland, shrub, heath, bare land	Water	Margin Estimated from the LUCAS Sample	
Artificial surfaces	13.4	0.7	0.7	6.5	0	0.4	1.8	3.3	0.4	27.2	27.9
Arable non irrigated cropland	3.3	40.8	10.1	8.7	0.7	1.1	2.5	3.3	1.1	71.6	65.2
Rice and arable irrigated cropland	0.7	2.2	0.7	0	0	0	0	0.4	0	4.0	4.3
Pastures	0	0.4	0.4	2.5	0	0	0	0.4	0	3.7	42.7
Natural grassland	0	0	0	1.8	0	0	0.4	2.2	0	4.4	14.4
Vineyards, fruits, arable permanent crops	1.1	5.4	2.5	4.0	4.0	11.9	1.4	4.3	1.1	35.7	9.0
Olive trees	2.2	1.8	1.1	2.5	25.3	1.8	2.2	4.7	0	41.6	10.1
Complex agricultural landscape	1.4	4.0	2.5	4.3	1.1	1.8	0.7	2.2	0.4	18.4	25.4
Agriculture, agroforestry, natural vegetation	7.6	7.6	0	0	0	0	45.9	7.6	0	68.7	22.1
Forest	0.4	0	0	0.4	0	0	11.9	1.4	0.4	14.5	69.5
Other natural vegetation, open spaces	0.7	0.4	0.4	9.4	0.7	0.4	11.9	28.9	1.1	53.9	53.1
Water and wetland	0.4	0	0	4.3	0	0	0.7	3.3	9.4	18.1	18.1
Margin Estimated from LUCAS Sample	31.2	63.3	18.4	44.4	31.8	17.4	79.4	62.0	13.9	361.8	361.8

25 ha in extent. Smaller forest patches are considered inclusions within a non-forest CORINE polygon, and likewise, a forest polygon may include undifferentiated non-forest inclusions. Also, classification criteria for forest cover in the CORINE system are less precise regarding crown cover and tree height. Gallego and Bamps describe other differences.

Regardless of their differences, there is a non-random association between the LUCAS-2001 and CORINE cross-classifications of SSUs (Table 1). Therefore, exhaustive information from the full-coverage CORINE land cover map potentially can serve as auxiliary data to improve LUCAS-2001 estimates. Columns in Table 1 represent classification of LUCAS-2001 SSUs with the LUCAS-2001 definitions and protocols. Rows represent the classification of LUCAS-2001 SSUs with the CORINE definitions, protocols, and GIS operator. The column margin is the estimated areal coverage of LUCAS-2001 land use categories in the population as estimated with the LUCAS-2001 sample alone. The row margin is the distribution of CORINE land cover categories estimated from the LUCAS-2001 sample. In addition, the same row margin is known exactly through the GIS enumeration of all CORINE polygons in the domain (Table 1). The difference between the sample estimate and census enumeration of the row margin is caused solely by random sampling errors in the LUCAS-2001 sample. RRE applies equality constraints (e.g., Simon and Chia 2002, Knottnerus 2003 p. 325) such that the RRE estimate of the row margin exactly equals the CORINE census value. In this sense, RRE may be considered calibrated to the auxiliary census statistics (Zhang 2000). The empirical correlations between the CORINE and LUCAS-2001 categorical variables, which are solely estimated from the LUCAS-2001 sample, improve statistical estimates of LUCAS-2001 categories using the CORINE census data as auxiliary constraints.

Census of CORINE Polygons

The rasterized CORINE land cover map is a full-coverage set of pixels. Each CORINE pixel is classified into one, and only one, of 12 categories[8] using remotely sensed data. If pixel k is classified as category r, then the rth element $[x_r]_k$ of the 12-by-1 vector x_k equals 1, while all remaining elements $[x_{i \neq r}]_k = 0$. Complete enumeration of all CORINE pixels in the analysis domain (U) yields the vector constant $\mathbf{t}_{CORINE}$, i.e., the exact population totals for remotely sensed auxiliary data from the CORINE land use map:

$$\mathbf{t}_{CORINE} = \sum_{k \in U} \begin{bmatrix} x_{r=1} \\ x_{r=2} \\ \vdots \\ x_{r=12} \end{bmatrix}_k = \sum_{k \in U} \mathbf{x}_k \tag{1}$$

The vector of population constants in Equation 1 serves as the "measurement vector" in the static Kalman filter (Maybeck 1979 p. 174, Knottnerus 2003 p. 50). It has a null 12-by-12 covariance matrix ($\mathbf{R} = \mathbf{0}$) because the census of CORINE pixels yields exact constants for population totals without sampling or enumeration errors.

Multivariate Sample Estimates of LUCAS-2001 Contingency Table

RRE can use a multivariate structure for the cross-classification of 9 LUCAS-2001 categories[9] and 12 CORINE categories[8] (Table 1). The LUCAS-2001 sample provides this ($12 \times 9 = 108$)-by-1 vector estimate of the 12-by-9 contingency table. It uses the ratio version of the multivariate Hansen-Horvitz estimator (Dryver 1999):

$$\left. \begin{aligned} \hat{\mathbf{t}}_{LUCAS} &= A\,\hat{\bar{\mathbf{z}}} \\ &= A \frac{\sum_{j=1}^{m} n_j \bar{\mathbf{z}}_j}{\sum_{j=1}^{m} n_j} \\ &= A \frac{\sum_{j=1}^{m} n_j \sum_{i=1}^{n_j} (\mathbf{z}_{ij}/n_j)}{\sum_{j=1}^{m} n_j} \\ &= \frac{A}{n} \sum_{j=1}^{m} \sum_{i=1}^{n_j} \mathbf{z}_{ji} \end{aligned} \right\} \quad \text{where} \quad \left\{ \begin{aligned} \mathbf{z}_{ji} &= \begin{bmatrix} z_{r=1 \cap q=1} \\ \vdots \\ z_{r=1 \cap q=9} \\ \vdots \\ z_{r=12 \cap q=1} \\ \vdots \\ z_{r=12 \cap q=9} \end{bmatrix}_{ji} \\ \bar{\mathbf{z}}_j &= \sum_{i=1}^{n_j} (\mathbf{z}_{ij}/n_j) \end{aligned} \right. \tag{2}$$

where $A = 361,800 \text{ km}^2$ is the total domain area (Table 1), $m = 1114$ is the number of LUCAS-2001 PSUs[7] in the domain, n_j is the number of SSUs in PSU j, $\mathbf{z}_{ij}$ is the 108-by-1 vector measurement of the ji^{th} SSU, and n is the total number of SSUs within the domain among all PSUs. Element $[z_{r \cap q}]_{ji}$ of $\mathbf{z}_{ij}$ equals 1 if SSU ji is classified as CORINE category r and LUCAS-2001 category q, while the remaining 107 elements of $\mathbf{z}_{ij}$ equal 0. Zhang (2000) labels this technique as "dummy indexing." Equation 2 is a multivariate version of the univariate ratio estimator, which Gallego and Bamps (2008) used within each of their four strata. The number of SSUs in PSU j (n_j) is the covariable and A/n is the SSU expansion factor. The estimator in Equation 2 is not stratified using auxiliary-variables, such as the CORINE land cover map. The population-vector estimate in Equation 2 is analogous to the "state-vector" estimate in the Kalman filter (Maybeck 1979, Knottnerus 2003 p. 50).

The 108-by-108 covariance matrix associated with Equation 2 is estimated as an ad hoc multivariate generalization of the model-based Matérn (1960) estimator for systematic sampling in two dimensions:

$$\hat{\mathbf{V}}\left(\hat{\mathbf{t}}_{\text{LUCAS}}\right) = A^2 \sum_{j=1}^{m} \frac{\sum_{j \neq j'} \left(n_j + n_{j'}\right)\delta_{jj'}\left(\dfrac{\overline{\mathbf{z}}_j}{n_j} - \hat{\overline{\mathbf{z}}}\right)\left(\dfrac{\overline{\mathbf{z}}_{j'}}{n_{j'}} - \hat{\overline{\mathbf{z}}}\right)'}{2\sum_{j \neq j'}\left(n_j + n_{j'}\delta_{jj'}\right)} \tag{3}$$

where j' indexes one of the eight nearest PSUs in geographic space to PSU j, and $\delta_{jj'}$ is the inverse geographic distance between the centroids of PSUs j and j'. Empirical tests by Gallego and Bamps suggest that the univariate version of Equation 3 is a nearly unbiased estimator of the sampling variance.

The estimated area for each land use category using the LUCAS-2001 protocol (i.e., column margin of Table 1) is the linear transformation of Equations 2 and 3 with the 9-by-108 indicator matrix $\mathbf{H}_y$ of zeros and ones:

$$\left(\hat{\mathbf{t}}_{\text{LUCAS}}\right)_y = \mathbf{H}_y\left(\hat{\mathbf{t}}_{\text{LUCAS}}\right) \tag{4}$$

$$\hat{\mathbf{V}}\left(\hat{\mathbf{t}}_{\text{LUCAS}}\right)_y = \mathbf{H}_y\left[\hat{\mathbf{V}}\left(\hat{\mathbf{t}}_{\text{LUCAS}}\right)\right]\mathbf{H}_y' \tag{5}$$

$$\mathbf{H}_y = \begin{bmatrix} 1 & 0 & \cdots & 0 & 1 & 0 & \cdots & 0 & \cdots & 1 & 0 & \cdots & 0 \\ 0 & 1 & \cdots & 0 & 0 & 1 & \cdots & 0 & \cdots & 0 & 1 & \cdots & 0 \\ \vdots & \vdots & \ddots & \vdots & \vdots & \vdots & \ddots & \vdots & \cdots & \vdots & \vdots & \ddots & \vdots \\ 0 & 0 & \cdots & 1 & 0 & 0 & \cdots & 1 & \cdots & 0 & 0 & \cdots & 1 \end{bmatrix} = \begin{bmatrix} \mathbf{I} & \mathbf{I} & \cdots & \mathbf{I} \end{bmatrix} = \mathbf{1} \otimes \mathbf{I} \tag{6}$$

where $\mathbf{I}$ is the 9-by-9 identity matrix, $\mathbf{1}$ is the 1-by-12 row matrix of 1's, and $\otimes$ denotes the Kronecker product. The ultimate goal with RRE is to improve the estimate in Equation 4 by reducing the size of the covariance matrix in Equation 5, where auxiliary census statistics from the CORINE map (Equation 1) are used to optimally constrain the design-consistent estimate in Equation 2.

The area for each CORINE category of land cover (i.e., row margin in Table 1) estimated from the LUCAS-2001 sample (Equation 2) equals the linear transformation

$$\left(\hat{\mathbf{t}}_{\text{LUCAS}}\right)_x = \mathbf{H}_x\left(\hat{\mathbf{t}}_{\text{LUCAS}}\right) \tag{7}$$

$$\hat{\mathbf{V}}\left(\hat{\mathbf{t}}_{\text{LUCAS}}\right)_x = \mathbf{H}_x\left[\hat{\mathbf{V}}\left(\hat{\mathbf{t}}_{\text{LUCAS}}\right)\right]\mathbf{H}_x' \tag{8}$$

$$\mathbf{H}_x = \begin{bmatrix} 1 & 1 & \cdots & 1 & 0 & 0 & \cdots & 0 & \cdots & 0 & 0 & \cdots & 0 \\ 0 & 0 & \cdots & 0 & 1 & 1 & \cdots & 1 & \cdots & 0 & 0 & \cdots & 0 \\ \vdots & \vdots & \ddots & \vdots & \vdots & \vdots & \ddots & \ddots & \cdots & \vdots & \vdots & \ddots & \vdots \\ 0 & 0 & \cdots & 0 & 0 & 0 & \cdots & 0 & \cdots & 1 & 1 & \cdots & 1 \end{bmatrix} = \begin{bmatrix} \mathbf{1} & \mathbf{0} & \cdots & \mathbf{0} \\ \mathbf{0} & \mathbf{1} & \cdots & \mathbf{0} \\ \vdots & \vdots & \ddots & \vdots \\ \mathbf{0} & \mathbf{0} & \cdots & \mathbf{1} \end{bmatrix} = \mathbf{I} \otimes \mathbf{1} \tag{9}$$

where $\mathbf{H}_x$ is a 12-by-108 indicator matrix, $\mathbf{1}$ is the 1-by-9 matrix of 1's, and $\mathbf{I}$ is the 12-by-12 identity matrix. Equations 7 and 9 respectively describe the "measurement vector" and the "measurement matrix" in the Kalman filter (Maybeck 1979 p. 114, Knottnerus 2003 p. 50). By design, Equations 2 and 7 are unbiased estimators, where the expected value is

$\text{E}\left[\mathbf{H}_x\hat{\mathbf{t}}_{\text{LUCAS}}\right] = \mathbf{t}_{\text{CORINE}}$. As a reminder, Equations 2 through 9 are estimators for the entire domain; they are not stratified.

The next step uses RRE to constrain the row margin of Table 1 to equal the census constants from the CORINE land cover map (Equation 1) such that the RRE estimates for the auxiliary-variables exactly agree with their exact population census values (i.e., constants):

$$\mathbf{H}_x\hat{\mathbf{t}}_{\text{RRE}} = \mathbf{t}_{\text{CORINE}} \tag{10}$$

Recursive Restriction Estimator (RRE)

The Recursive Restriction Estimator (RRE) is equivalent to the multivariate composite estimator, which Gregoire and Walters (1988) characterize as an extension of the univariate composite estimator. The latter has been used in forest inventory and monitoring applications for nearly 50 years (e.g., sampling with partial replacement by Bickford and others 1963). In the following discourse, RE refers to the Restriction Estimator as a single recursion within the sequential RRE.

The univariate composite estimator combines two independent estimates by weighting each inversely proportional to their variances[10]. Diderrich (1985) and Gregoire and Walters demonstrate the algebraic equivalence of the multivariate RE with the mixed estimator (Theil and Goldberger 1961). Knottnerus (2003) makes a strong connection among the multivariate static Kalman filter, Pythagorean regression, and Generalized Least Squares estimators in the context of complex sample surveys. RE is algebraically identical to a Bayes estimator (e.g., Jazwinski 1970 p. 145, Maybeck 1979 p. 205); the minimum mean square error predictor (e.g., Jazwinski, 1970 p. 149, Maybeck 1979 p. 232, Knottnerus 2003 p. 50, Chui and

Chen 2009 p. 21); and the maximum likelihood estimator when joint densities are all Gaussian (e.g., Jazwinski 1970 p. 207, Maybeck 1979 p. 234, Binder and Hidiroglou 1988 p. 200, Knottnerus 2003 p. 28).

RE combines two vector estimates with the weighting matrix $\mathbf{K}$:

$$\hat{\mathbf{t}}_{RE} = \mathbf{K}\,\mathbf{t}_{CORINE} + \left(\mathbf{I} - \mathbf{K}\mathbf{H}_x\right)\hat{\mathbf{t}}_{LUCAS} \tag{11}$$

$\mathbf{K}$ is the 108-by-12 matrix weight placed on the 12-by-1 CORINE census vector $\mathbf{t}_{CORINE}$, and $(\mathbf{I}-\mathbf{K}\mathbf{H}_x)$ is the 108-by-108 matrix weight placed on the 108-by-1 sample vector estimate from LUCAS-2001. Equation 11 has the structure of a composite estimator (Särndal and others 1992 p. 371). The following algebraic identity has the structure of the generalized regression estimator (Särndal and others 1992 p. 225, Carfagna and Gallego 2005) and Pythagorean regression (Knottnerus 2003 p. 30):

$$\hat{\mathbf{t}}_{RE} = \hat{\mathbf{t}}_{LUCAS} + \mathbf{K}\left(\mathbf{t}_{CORINE} - \mathbf{H}_x\hat{\mathbf{t}}_{LUCAS}\right) \tag{12}$$

To maximize efficiency, the weighting matrix $\mathbf{K}$ is derived with either linear least squares or Gaussian maximum likelihood optimality criteria (Maybeck 1979 p. 120 and 234, Diderrich 1985, Gregoire and Walters 1988, Simon and Chia 2002, Knottnerus 2003 p. 31):

$$\mathbf{K} = \hat{\mathbf{V}}\left(\hat{\mathbf{t}}_{LUCAS}\right)\mathbf{H}_x'\left[\mathbf{H}_x\,\hat{\mathbf{V}}\left(\hat{\mathbf{t}}_{LUCAS}\right)\mathbf{H}_x' + \mathbf{R}\right]^{-1} \tag{13}$$

where $\mathbf{R}$ is the covariance matrix for the measurement vector (Equation 7). The resulting covariance matrix of RE is

$$\hat{\mathbf{V}}\left(\hat{\mathbf{t}}_{RE}\right) = \mathbf{K}\mathbf{R}\mathbf{K}' + \left(\mathbf{I} - \mathbf{K}\mathbf{H}_x\right)\left[\hat{\mathbf{V}}\left(\hat{\mathbf{t}}_{LUCAS}\right)\right]\left(\mathbf{I} - \mathbf{K}\mathbf{H}_x\right)' \tag{14}$$

Recall that the 12-by-12 covariance matrix $\mathbf{R} = \mathbf{0}$ for the 12-by-1 vector of census constants $\mathbf{t}_{CORINE}$ (Equation 1). Given this identity, plus the definition in Equation 8, Equations 13 and 14 reduce to

$$\mathbf{K} = \hat{\mathbf{V}}\left(\hat{\mathbf{t}}_{LUCAS}\right)\mathbf{H}_x'\left[\mathbf{H}_x\,\hat{\mathbf{V}}\left(\hat{\mathbf{t}}_{LUCAS}\right)\mathbf{H}_x'\right]^{-1} \tag{15}$$

$$\hat{\mathbf{V}}\left(\hat{\mathbf{t}}_{RE}\right) = \left(\mathbf{I} - \mathbf{K}\mathbf{H}_x\right)\hat{\mathbf{V}}\left(\hat{\mathbf{t}}_{LUCAS}\right)\left(\mathbf{I} - \mathbf{K}\mathbf{H}_x\right)' \tag{16}$$

Simon and Chia (2002) prove that the 108-by-1 RE in Equation 11 satisfies the 12-by-1 vector constraint in Equation 10, the RE is unbiased, and the RE has a smaller error covariance than the unconstrained vector estimator in Equations 2 and 4. Czaplewski (2010) demonstrates that the diagonal partition of the covariance matrix for the CORINE variables in Equation 16 is null (i.e., $\mathbf{R} = \mathbf{0}$), and the off-diagonal cross-correlation partition between the LUCAS-2001 study-variables and the CORINE auxiliary census variables is likewise null. Therefore, the RE vector estimate is independent of the CORINE auxiliary-variables, i.e., the RE "filters-out" all relevant information from the CORINE census.

The CORINE census information is no longer needed after it is assimilated by the RE. This is an example of the "memoryless" attribute of the Kalman filter (Kalman and others 1969). This not only reduces the dimensions of the static state-space for more complex sampling designs, it also simplifies updating expansion values in a large statistical database as new data are acquired (Czaplewski 2010). Furthermore, the estimated covariance matrix in Equation 16 is unbiased (conditional upon the sample) and is not an approximation, as with PS (e.g., Cochran 1977 p. 135, Särndal and others 1992 p. 266, Scott and others 2005). However, proof of these characteristics assumes that the covariance matrix in the partition for the

CORINE variables in the LUCAS-2001 sample, i.e., $\mathbf{H}_x \hat{\mathbf{V}}\left(\hat{\mathbf{t}}_{\text{LUCAS}}\right) \mathbf{H}'_x$ in Equation 15, is full rank. Since the vector estimate in Equation 7 exactly sums to constant A (Equation 2), its covariance matrix in Equation 8 is positive-semidefinite, i.e., not full rank. In this case, one of the 12 constraints in Equation 7 is redundant. The next section addresses this mathematical nuisance.

Numerically Robust Algorithm

Equations 11 to 16 are notoriously vulnerable to numerical round-off errors as the measurement error covariance matrix becomes small, i.e., $\mathbf{R} \rightarrow \mathbf{0}$. Bierman (1977) wrote an entire treatise on the subject, and entire chapters of seminal books on the Kalman filter are devoted to it (e.g., Maybeck 1979, Bar-Shalom and others 2001, Grewal and Andrews 2001, Chui and Chen 2009). A slightly different algorithm is feasible even with a positive-semidefinite covariance matrix (Equation 9). Since the constraints are constants with a null covariance matrix (i.e., $\mathbf{R} = \mathbf{0}$), they are mutually independent by definition, and each scalar element of the constraint vector in Equation 7 may be applied separately in a sequential recursive algorithm (Knottnerus 2003 p. 346).

Let $\mathbf{h}_i$ be the 1-by-108 vector containing row i of the measurement matrix $\mathbf{H}_x$. The estimator that sequentially applies all 12 scalar constraints, $i = \{1,2,\ldots,12\}$, is defined as

$$\left(\hat{\mathbf{t}}_{\text{RRE}}\right)_i = \left(\hat{\mathbf{t}}_{\text{RRE}}\right)_{i-1} + \mathbf{k}_i \left[\left(t_{\text{CORINE}}\right)_i - \mathbf{h}_i \left(\hat{\mathbf{t}}_{\text{RRE}}\right)_{i-1}\right] \tag{17}$$

$$\hat{\mathbf{V}}\left(\hat{\mathbf{t}}_{\text{RRE}}\right)_i = \left(\mathbf{I} - \mathbf{k}_i \mathbf{h}_i\right)\left[\hat{\mathbf{V}}\left(\hat{\mathbf{t}}_{\text{RRE}}\right)_{i-1}\right]\left(\mathbf{I} - \mathbf{k}_i \mathbf{h}_i\right)' \tag{18}$$

$$\mathbf{k}_i = \left(\frac{1}{\mathbf{h}_i \hat{\mathbf{V}}\left(\hat{\mathbf{t}}_{\text{RRE}}\right)_{i-1} \mathbf{h}'_i}\right)\hat{\mathbf{V}}\left(\hat{\mathbf{t}}_{\text{RRE}}\right)_{i-1} \mathbf{h}'_i \tag{19}$$

where $\mathbf{k}_i$ is the 108-by-1 column vector of optimal weights and $(t_{\text{CORINE}})_i$ is the ith element of the constraint vector $\mathbf{t}_{\text{CORINE}}$. At the first step in this recursive sequence, $i = 1$, $(i-1) = 0$, $(\hat{\mathbf{t}}_{\text{RRE}})_0 = (\hat{\mathbf{t}}_{\text{RE}})_0 = \hat{\mathbf{t}}_{\text{LUCAS}}$ from Equation 2, and $\hat{\mathbf{V}}(\hat{\mathbf{t}}_{\text{RRE}})_0 = \hat{\mathbf{V}}(\hat{\mathbf{t}}_{\text{LUCAS}})$ from Equation 3. After applying the 12 CORINE census constraints, the final RRE equals

$$\left(\hat{\mathbf{t}}_{\text{RRE}}\right)_{12} = \left(\hat{\mathbf{t}}_{\text{LUCAS}}\right) + \sum_{i=1}^{12} \mathbf{k}_i \left[\left(t_{\text{CORINE}}\right)_i - \mathbf{h}_i \left(\hat{\mathbf{t}}_{\text{RRE}}\right)_{i-1}\right] \tag{20}$$

$$\hat{\mathbf{V}}\left(\hat{\mathbf{t}}_{\text{RRE}}\right)_{12} = \left(\prod_{i=\{12,11,\cdots,1\}}\left(\mathbf{I} - \mathbf{k}_i \mathbf{h}_i\right)\right)\hat{\mathbf{V}}\left(\hat{\mathbf{t}}_{\text{LUCAS}}\right)\left(\prod_{i=\{1,2,\cdots,12\}}\left(\mathbf{I} - \mathbf{k}_i \mathbf{h}_i\right)'\right) \tag{21}$$

The 108-by-1 RRE vector estimate in Equation 20 is more efficient for the entire 12-by-9 contingency table (Table 1) than the unconstrained estimator in Equation 2 (Simon and Chia 2002). It can be seen as the Gram-Schmidt orthogonalization of Equation 11 (Knottnerus 2003 p. 346). The 12-by-1 row margin of CORINE estimates from RRE (Equation 10) will exactly equal the equality constraints from the CORINE census (Equation 1).

The sum of all elements in the vector $\mathbf{t}_{\mathrm{CORINE}}$ and the corresponding partition of the state vector $\left(\mathbf{H}_x \hat{\mathbf{t}}_{\mathrm{LUCAS}}\right)$ exactly equal the total area in the population, i.e., the constant A in Equations 2 and 3. Therefore, one auxiliary-variable is "redundant" (Zhang 2000), and the partition of the state-vector covariance matrix for the auxiliary variables $\mathbf{H}_x \hat{\mathbf{V}}\left(\hat{\mathbf{t}}_{\mathrm{LUCAS}}\right)\mathbf{H}_x'$ is positive-semidefinite, i.e., the matrix inverse of $\mathbf{H}_x \hat{\mathbf{V}}\left(\hat{\mathbf{t}}_{\mathrm{LUCAS}}\right)\mathbf{H}_x'$ in Equation 16 is not feasible. The linear calibration estimator and the general regression estimator (GREG) require omission of the redundant variable (Zhang 2000). A similar solution could be applied to the RE in Equation 16, although this solution might not be numerically robust. On the other hand, the RRE algorithm in Equations 20 and 21 uses scalar inverses, not a matrix inverse. In fact, the RRE algorithm requires sequential processing of all 12 CORINE variables to utilize fully all information in the auxiliary census statistics, even if the vector $\left(\mathbf{H}_x \hat{\mathbf{t}}_{\mathrm{LUCAS}}\right)$ includes redundant elements.

In the inventory context, the RRE column margin statistics represent the optimal estimates of the LUCAS variables. These are computed through linear transformations of Equations 20 and 21 with the 9-by-108 indicator matrix H_y, which is defined in Equation 6:

$$\left(\hat{\mathbf{t}}_{\mathrm{RRE}}\right)_y = \mathbf{H}_y \left(\hat{\mathbf{t}}_{\mathrm{RRE}}\right) \tag{22}$$

$$\hat{\mathbf{V}}\left(\hat{\mathbf{t}}_{\mathrm{RRE}}\right)_y = \mathbf{H}_y \left[\hat{\mathbf{V}}\left(\hat{\mathbf{t}}_{\mathrm{RRE}}\right)\right]\mathbf{H}_y' \tag{23}$$

When census constants are imposed as constraints, RRE in Equations 17 to 21 is numerically more efficient than the usual estimators in Equations 11 to 16 (Maybeck 1979 p. 375, Grewal and Andrews 2001 p. 226). Perhaps more important, RRE is more easily implemented in database software[11] because it replaces a matrix inversion with a more numerically robust sequence of scalar inverses.

Residual Analysis

Analysis of the residual differences between census statistics and their sample estimates can reveal otherwise obscure anomalies, such as substantial numerical errors. There is precedence in sample survey applications. Estevao and Särndal (2006) recommend residual analysis to understand better how complex auxiliary information reduces variance. Gallego and Bamps (2008) use residual analysis between CORINE census statistics and LUCAS-2001 estimates to gain confidence in Matérn's model-based variance estimator for systematic sampling. Coulston (2008) uses residual analysis to detect procedural anomalies with FIA photo-interpretation procedures used in PS.

One simple analysis of the sequential RRE standardizes each scalar residual by dividing it by an estimate of its expected standard deviation:

$$r_i = \frac{t_i - \mathbf{h}_i \left(\hat{\mathbf{t}}_{RRE} \right)_{i-1}}{\sqrt{\mathbf{h}_i \hat{\mathbf{V}} \left(\hat{\mathbf{t}}_{RRE} \right)_{i-1} \mathbf{h}_i'}} \tag{24}$$

Each standardized scalar residual is expected to have zero mean and unit variance and to be mutually independent of all other residuals (Maybeck 1979 p. 229, Knottnerus 2003 p. 38). If there are no substantial round-off errors or other anomalies, then the realized distribution of the standardized residual series will be consistent with these expectations.

For example, there are 12 residuals in the Gallego and Bamps (2008) case study (Equations 17 to 21 and 24), and the hypotheses of zero mean and unit variance may be empirically tested using familiar univariate methods in parametric and nonparametric statistics. Other tests might use residuals at the PSU level (Knottnerus 2003 p. 255, Czaplewski 2010).

Results

The case study, which is based on Gallego and Bamps (2008), is solely intended as a hypothetical example. However, the results from this case study further illuminate differences between PS and RRE. Figure 1 compares efficiencies of the post-stratified estimator and RRE relative to systematic sampling without remotely sensed CORINE data. Values equal to 1 signify estimates that do not gain efficiency from the CORINE data, i.e., the level of uncertainty from the LUCAS-2001 sample alone without remotely sensed auxiliary information. Values closer to 0 are more efficient, i.e., low uncertainty. Differences in statistical efficiency are caused by the different ways in which the remotely sensed CORINE data are used with PS and RRE. The PS estimate uses 4 strata developed by Gallego and Bamps with CORINE data to describe agricultural prevalence within each 90-ha LUCAS-2001 PSU, whereas RRE directly uses all 12 CORINE categories of land cover (Table 1) for each 0.0009-ha LUCAS-2001 SSU.

Both estimators are at least as efficient as the systematic sampling estimator alone (Figure 1). Simon and Chia (2002) prove this is always true for RRE, although this is not necessarily true with PS (Cochran 1977 p. 99, Czaplewski and Patterson 2003). RRE produces substantially smaller standard deviations (Figure 1) for forest, woodland, shrub, heath, bare land, and temporary pastures and fallow fields. The post-stratified estimates have smaller standard deviations for the remaining land use categories. Overall, RRE is more efficient, with a square root trace of its error covariance matrix that is nearly half that of the post-stratified estimate. The post-stratified estimate uses prevalence of agricultural use within each 90-ha PSU, which might explain the somewhat higher accuracy of PS for the agricultural land uses.

Figure 2 displays the results of a residual analysis[12]. Two of the 12 residuals differ from 0 by over 3 standard deviation units. Such relatively extreme deviations are not normally expected if all assumptions used in this example for RRE are correct. While this rare anomaly could merely be a chance event, the most likely suspect is a poor estimate of the covariance

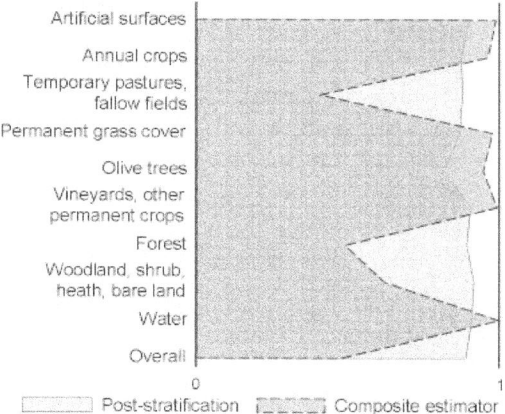

Relative Estimation Error for LUCAS Variables

Artificial surfaces
Annual crops
Temporary pastures, fallow fields
Permanent grass cover
Olive trees
Vineyards, other permanent crops
Forest
Woodland, shrub, heath, bare land
Water
Overall

0   1

Post-stratification   Composite estimator

Figure 1. Standard deviations for post-stratified and RRE estimates of LUCAS-2001 land use categories relative to systematic sampling alone. A value equal to 1 indicates no improvement with remotely sensed CORINE auxiliary data, and 0 equals perfect accuracy

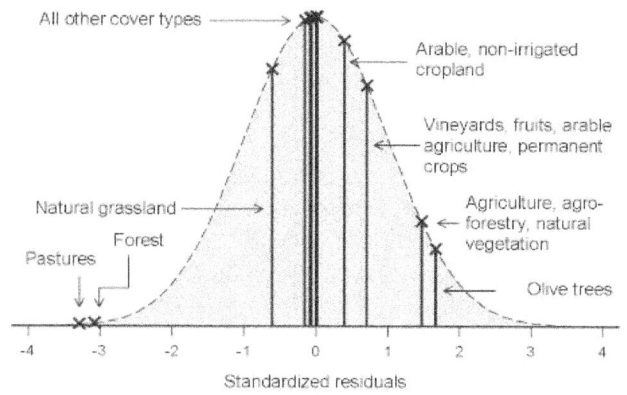

Distribution of CORINE Residuals

All other cover types
Arable, non-irrigated cropland
Vineyards, fruits, arable agriculture, permanent crops
Natural grassland
Agriculture, agro-forestry, natural vegetation
Forest
Pastures
Olive trees

-4   -3   -2   -1   0   1   2   3   4

Standardized residuals

Figure 2. Standardized residuals from Restriction estimator (RRE). Assuming a Gaussian distribution with zero mean and unit variance12, two CORINE residuals appear unlikely given the underlying assumptions: pastures and forest cover types. The suspected cause is an inaccurate estimate of the covariance matrix from the LUCAS-2001 sample. Residual analysis is an important component of RRE.

matrix for the systematic LUCAS-2001 sample. The case study used numerous assumptions to reconstruct this covariance matrix (Appendix A) because the realized sample covariance matrix is not reported by Gallego and Bamps. Therefore, results from this case study cannot be reliably inferred to that study. Although not shown in Figure 2, residual analysis of the usual formulation of RRE with vector constraints (Equations 11, 15, and 16) revealed one implausibly large residual. This indicates substantial numerical round-off errors with the usual Kalman filter algorithm, which is a well-known hazard (Bierman 1977, Maybeck 1979). The sequential estimator in Equations 17 to 21 is more numerically robust.

Discussion

Knottnerus (2003) drew the first strong connection among sampling theory, regression theory, and systems theory. All three are mature theories in statistics, but systems theory is not widely known within the sample survey discipline. Knottnerus makes extensive references to the Kalman filter[13] from the perspective of Pythagorean regression in the sample survey context. Knottnerus (2003 p. viii) views this as a "constrained estimation problem ... identical to the solution of an ordinary unconstrained linear least squares problem with the unconstrained estimator as dependent regressand, the set of constraints as regressors, and the constrained estimator as an orthogonal residual." Knottnerus' standard sampling model views the world as a finite set of population elements, and RRE combines separate estimates for all elements in the population.

As a somewhat subtle distinction, my use of RRE views the world as a state-vector for an infinite-population. The state-vector includes both field study-variables and remotely sensed auxiliary-variables. The remotely sensed census of pixels is used as auxiliary measurement information to improve the estimated state-vector. In fact, the improvement is "perfect" in that the RRE estimate for auxiliary-variables agrees exactly with the corresponding census constants. The RRE estimate of the study-variables in the state-vector is improved through the sample cross-covariance matrix between the study-variables and auxiliary-variables. The infinite-population perspective can be simpler (Mandallaz 2008 p. 61) and arguably more natural for continuous spatial populations, such as those considered by FIA and LUCAS-2001.

PS requires cross-classification of all categorical auxiliary census variables, which multiplicatively increases the number of strata (Zhang 2000). However, the feasible limit to the number of strata is determined by sample size of PSUs, which constrains the degree to which otherwise useful auxiliary information can improve statistical efficiency with PS (Mandallaz 2008 p. 89). Knottnerus (2003 p. 169) addresses this problem through a two-stage estimator for a finite-population where strata are considered clusters and estimates of first- and second-order inclusion probabilities are necessary. In principle, calibration estimation based on marginal totals for a finite-population also avoids the need to collapse empty post-strata into more prevalent strata (Zhang 2000). This is also known as generalized raking (Deville and others 1993), which can be unstable or can fail to converge (Zhang 2000).

RRE also can be structured to avoid problems associated with cross-classification. Under the infinite-population model, RRE sequentially assimilates information from multiple polychotomous auxiliary-variables without requiring cross-classification or estimation of joint inclusion probabilities. For example, Equations 17 to 21 impose constraints based on the set of CORINE classifications for 0.0009-ha SSUs in the LUCAS-2001 sample. Those RRE results can be further constrained with a second set of census statistics, such as the four categories of agricultural extent within each 90-ha PSU used by Gallego and Bamps for PS. Combination of these two sets of constraints with RRE is expected to improve accuracy, especially for agricultural land uses (Figure 1). A third set of constraints might use geopolitical boundaries such as individual EU15 nations. Other auxiliary geospatial variables might include ecofloristic zones, land forms, and land ownership. More details follow.

The PS estimator assumes each PSU is a member of one, and only one, stratum (Särndal and others 1992 p. 264). This compelled Gallego and Bamps (2008) to collapse 44 remotely sensed CORINE categories into four strata where each 90-ha LUCAS-2001 PSU in the domain is assigned to one, and only one, stratum. Since RRE incorporates auxiliary census data as constraints rather than through stratification, the full classification system of 44 CORINE categories could be used for each

0.0009-ha LUCAS-2001 SSU. Furthermore, RRE avoids concerns raised by McRoberts (2005) and Van Deusen (2005) with the FIA variance estimator (Scott and others 2005), which assumes independence among post-strata (see also Breidt and Opsomer 2008).

The case study uses categorical auxiliary-variables to contrast RRE with PS. However, RRE may also utilize continuous variables as auxiliary census constraints. After all, the regression estimator is equivalent to PS with H strata when the auxiliary-variable consists of H categories in a polychotomous variable, i.e., H dichotomous "dummy" variables (Knottnerus 2003 p. 130). For example, RRE can directly use the proportion of agriculture from the CORINE map in each 90-ha LUCAS PSU as a continuous auxiliary-variable. Gallego and Bamps' transformation of this continuous variable into four categorical levels is unnecessary with RRE. The continuous variable would require one element in the state-vector rather than four dichotomous variables for the categorical variable. Other continuous auxiliary-variables could also serve as census constraints. Examples include climatic variables (e.g., annual number of frost-free days), human population density, road density, and crop production statistics. A continuous auxiliary-variable may be expressed as interpolated geospatial surface (e.g., Tomppo and Halme 2004, Blackard and others 2008), or it may be summarized for each discrete cell in a tessellated surface, such as the 90-ha LUCAS cluster plot or a 2400-ha FIA hexagon (Reams and others 2005a). To increase the correlation with a study-variable, a continuous auxiliary-variable, such as tasseled cap transformation of remotely sensed multispectral data (e.g., Healey and others 2005), may be segregated by a categorical auxiliary-variable, such as soil type (e.g., Katila and Tomppo 2001). Continuous variables should be re-scaled to share a common spread, which reduces numerical problems (Maybeck 1979 p. 369, Bierman 1977 p. 15). As with any categorical auxiliary-variable, each continuous auxiliary-variable may be sequentially processed as a scalar constant with the RRE.

With stratification, the auxiliary-variable should be strongly correlated with the study-variable (Cochran 1977 p. 101). However, large surveys such as FIA and LUCAS study many different variables, and there is seldom a single auxiliary-variable that is universally well correlated with all study-variables (Särndal and others 1992 p. 100, Mandallaz 2008 p. 16). Unlike stratification, RRE applies scalar census constraints one at a time, and the classification system for remotely sensed data need not be composed of mutually exclusive and exhaustive categories. For example, a separate dichotomous thematic map can be optimized for each individual category of land cover, which can increase statistical efficiency with remotely sensed data (King 2002, Czaplewski and Patterson 2003). RRE can use a suite of different auxiliary-variables, each of which is optimized for different sets of study-variables. For example, geospatial interpolations of human population density might improve estimates of species diversity and wildlife habitat, while remotely sensed indices might improve estimates of biomass and merchantable wood volume.

Heinl and others (2009) conclude that "definition and selection of land cover classes (is) crucial and not to be simply adaptable from existing land cover class schemes. A stronger research focus toward discriminating land cover classes by their typical spectral, topographic, or seasonal properties is therefore suggested to advance image classification." RRE may use categorical auxiliary-variables with a classification scheme that differs from that used for the study-variables. An example is auxiliary data from the CORINE classification system for remotely sensed thematic mapping to improve study-variables as defined by the LUCAS classification system (Table 1). The important criterion is the strength of association between auxiliary- and study-variables (Mandallaz 2008 p. 16). Czaplewski and Patterson (2003) recommend that a single homogeneous forest condition (i.e., study-variable) should represent at least 70 percent of a remotely sensed stratum (i.e., categorical auxiliary-variable), and this recommendation might be useful with RRE.

Independent, remotely sensed thematic maps might be available from more than one time period, and annual change-detection maps are becoming more routine (e.g., Healey and others 2005, Sader and others 2005). The census statistic for each variable in a geospatial dataset may be recursively applied as an independent constraint. This obviates the advantage of a single, remotely sensed thematic map for PS in longitudinal panel surveys, as advocated by Van Deusen (2005).

Efficiency gains from remotely sensed auxiliary data depend strongly on the associations and correlations between field measurements and remotely sensed measurements (Cochran 1977 p. 101). Those associations are degraded by misregistration (Schowengerdt 2007 p. 356) between sites measured in the field and those same sites measured with remote sensing (Czaplewski and Patterson 2001, 2003). This problem is especially hazardous in heterogeneous, fine-grained landscapes. See Halme and Tomppo (2001), Czaplewski (2005), and Nelson and others (2009) for methods to improve registration accuracy. In addition, remotely sensed measurements may be accurate in certain situations but inaccurate in others. For example, the dense interior of forest stands and the open interior of cultivated agricultural fields can be accurately classified with remote sensing. However, sparse forest generation, idle agricultural fields, and forest edges can be difficult to classify accurately. Efficiency can be improved by separating sites with high measurement error into separate categories (e.g., Czaplewski and Patterson 2001, McRoberts and others 2002).

As auxiliary-variables are added to improve efficiency or impose geopolitical areal constraints, the dimensions of RRE state-vector become larger. This "curse of dimensionality" incurs numerical risks, such as imprecise estimates of the covariances and cross-covariances (Ledoit and Wolf 2004) used in Equations 16 and 19 to compute optimal weights for auxiliary data. However, categorical variables need not be cross-classified with RRE. For example, the $(12 \times 9 = 108)$-by-1 LUCAS-2001 vector z_{ji} in Equation 2 may be replaced with the concatenation of the margins of Table 1, resulting in a much smaller $(12 + 9 = 21)$-by-1 vector. This sacrifices any useful information available within the interior of the contingency table (Table 1). The resulting estimator might be sub-optimal but more numerically robust. However, the loss in statistical efficiency can be minor, as with many applications of the Kalman-Schmidt filter (e.g., Jazwinski 1970 p. 285, Grewal and Andrews 2001 p. 309, Knottnerus 2003 p. 371) and three-phase sampling (Magnussen 2003). In other applications where the PSU is a homogeneous point plot, the multinomial distribution[14] applies and the margin vectors are sufficient statistics for RRE (Appendix B). In this special case, there is no loss of efficiency by concatenation of the margins to avoid cross-classification (Knottnerus

2003 p. 367). Regardless, the RRE can avoid cross-classification of auxiliary variables, which creates empty sample post-strata (Zhang 2000).

Large government survey programs express estimators as PSU-level weights or "expansion factors." These modify the design-weights to capture information in the auxiliary-variables (Deville and Särndal 1992). The PSU weights simplify estimation within a large database and they are popular with analysts (Knottnerus 2003 p. 391, Scott and others 2005, Estevao and Särndal 2006, Mandallaz 2008 p. 45). In an analogous fashion, complex results from RRE may be simply expressed as PSU-level weights (i.e., multivariate expansion values) for population estimates and their associate variance estimates (Knottnerus 2003 p. 395, Czaplewski 2010). Sõstra and Traat (2009) use Knottnerus' RE to derive simpler scalar weights that depend solely on the auxiliary variables, i.e., the same multiplicative scalar weight applies to all study variables measured at a sampled PSU. However, the weights developed by Sõstra and Traat are sub-optimal, meaning they do not replicate the minimum variance linear estimator. Regardless, in one way or another, the results from RRE can be incorporated into the survey database as weights at the PSU-level, similar to current FIA methods that capture PS results as expansion factors (McRoberts 1999).

As a form of the static Kalman filter, RRE is capable of multivariate estimation of study-variables (e.g., Maybeck 1979), which facilitates compatible non-linear pseudo-estimators (Särndal and others 1992 pp.173-174, 205-207). Czaplewski (2010) uses pseudo-estimators for synthetic estimation (e.g., Purcell and Kish 1979), missing data imputation (e.g., Verbeke and Molenberghs 2000 p. 221), and consistent calibration for measurement error bias (e.g., Bound and others 2001). More important, RRE strengthens the connection to extensive engineering literature on Kalman filtering applications. The engineering perspective contributes essential solutions to numerical problems with the Kalman filter. These same numerical problems have posed a stubborn obstacle to optimal estimation in the sample survey estimation (e.g., Estevao and Särndal 2004 p. 657). Reliable applications of RRE are not feasible without robust algorithms and residual analysis.

Limitations from the finite sample size of PSUs cannot be ignored during the pursuit of efficiency through auxiliary-variables. The curse of dimensionality is a powerful foe. Numerous remotely sensed and other geospatial variables may be combined into mathematical models (e.g., Schowengerdt 2007 p. 387) that predict a few auxiliary-variables, such as forest type and biomass. These latter auxiliary-variables may be used to reduce the number of constraints in RRE. However, this produces a different complication with independence of model predictions and the realized sample (Breidt and Opsomer 2008). Regardless, auxiliary-variables should be highly associated or well correlated with at least one important study-variable. As a fail-safe, analysis of residuals might detect overzealous use of auxiliary-variables.

The variance estimator for PS is an approximation (although the bias introduced by the approximation is considered small, Särndal and others 1992 p. 267). Furthermore, this approximation assumes simple random sampling. Ad hoc assumptions are needed to apply this approximation with Matérn's model-based variance estimator for systematic sampling. On the other hand, RRE remains unbiased for variance estimation, conditional upon an unbiased estimator of the sampling error covariance matrix, and RRE does not need ad hoc assumptions for systematic sampling. Systematic sampling is widely used in surveys of forest and agricultural lands (Mandallaz 2008 p. 27), and accurate variance estimates with systematic sampling better characterize the true reliability of these expensive surveys.

Fattorini and others (2004) recognized the connection between multivariate two-phase sample survey estimators and accuracy assessment in remote sensing studies (see also Knottnerus 2003 p. 364). An accuracy assessment frequently uses a contingency table, which may also be termed an "error matrix" or "confusion matrix" in the remote sensing literature. Gallego and Bamps use the term "fine scale profiles" for a rectangular contingency table in which different classification systems are used with the reference and remotely sensed data (e.g., Table 1). Individual cells in the contingency table are estimated from the probability sample of reference plots, each of which is jointly classified with remote sensing and a more accurate reference protocol. Sampling error in the estimated contingency table may be reduced with RRE by constraining the marginal estimates of the remotely sensed categories to agree exactly with their known census values from the full-coverage thematic map[4]. In special cases, stratification on the remotely sensed categories sometimes achieves the same outcome (Congalton 1991). However, stratification becomes complicated with a heterogeneous cluster plot and whenever there are revisions to the remotely sensed categorical variable previously used for pre-stratification (Stehman and Czaplewski 1998). RRE remains feasible regardless of these complications. Czaplewski (1994) used pseudo-estimators (Särndal 1992 p. 173) to derive generalized variance formulae for common accuracy assessment statistics. These estimators use any reliable covariance matrix for a vectorized contingency table, regardless of the sampling design or estimator. (This capability demonstrates the value of multivariate formulations of sample survey estimators.)

With RRE, individual cell estimates in an error matrix can be negative, especially for rare cross-classifications. If the sole objective is estimation of the margin for the study-variables (e.g., LUCAS-2001 in Table 1), then negative cells are not a concern. If the objective is accuracy assessment or if a rare marginal element has a negative estimate, then Doran (1997), Simon and Chia (2002), and Knottnerus (2003 p. 379) present inequality constraints that can preclude negative estimates with RRE.

Equations 17 to 21 provide an example of sequential application of RRE for elements of a single series of land cover classifications. The discussion covers additional series of auxiliary census variables that deserve consideration. These series all produce vector constants (i.e., $R = 0$ in Equations 13 and 14). In addition, RRE can accommodate auxiliary measurements that are sample estimates (i.e., $R \neq 0$ in Equations 13 and 14). Coulston (2008) and Frescino and others (2009) provide FIA examples. A multistage design can use a census of remotely sensed variables at Stage One, a sample of more accurate and detailed remotely sensed data for cluster plots at Stage Two, and a sub-sample of field measurements within each cluster plot at Stage Three. The initial application of RRE can combine Stages One and Two into a more efficient population-vector estimate for the Stage Two variables. These RRE estimates can then be input into RRE, which improves population estimates for Stage Three field measurements.

Knottnerus (2003) and Czaplewski (2010) provide details and approaches to these and other complex sample survey estimators. In addition, the Kalman filter, which is a generalization of RRE, is a dynamic time-series estimator. It uses recursive least squares to conveniently and efficiently combine simple components of a complex estimator (Duncan and Horn 1972, Wolter 1979, Diderrich 1985, Knottnerus 2003 p. 39). Therefore, the Kalman filter offers a robust and unified approach to combining administrative data with multiple time-series of auxiliary remotely sensed data and time-series of panel data measured in the field.

Both RRE and PS estimators assume the auxiliary-variables are independent of the random errors from the sample of PSUs. However, those same PSUs are often used as "training data" to fit "supervised classifiers" or regression models that predict land characteristics (i.e., a thematic map) with remotely sensed and other geospatial data as predictor variables. Abundant examples appear in the remote sensing literature. Today's modeling tools include classification and regression trees (e.g., Blackard and others 2008), k-nearest neighbor non-parametric regression (e.g., Tomppo 2002), and artificial neural networks (e.g., Mas and Flores 2008). However, this modeling connection breaks the assumed independence among PSU auxiliary-variables; a different sample would produce a slightly different thematic map. It is commonly assumed that this dependence is small and can be ignored. Breidt and Opsomer (2008) provide some objective support for this assumption. However, this assumption is unnecessary if the geospatial variables are directly used without fitting a prediction model with PSU data. Examples of truly independent geospatial auxiliary-variables include the Normalized Difference Vegetation Index (e.g., Carlson and Ripley 1997) and the Tassel Cap (e.g., Healey and others 2005) transformations of remotely sensed multispectral data; physiographic variables derived from Digital Elevation Models; isopleths for climatic variables; ecoregion classifications; and landownership and geopolitical entities. Likewise, unsupervised classification (e.g., Vogelmann and others 1998) does not directly use the sampled PSUs. Pixel-level predictions from complex models should be used as auxiliary data only if they yield significantly more efficient estimates of the study-variables.

Conclusions

The Recursive Restriction Estimator (RRE) offers novel opportunities to improve the efficiency and accuracy of detailed sample survey statistics with remotely sensed and other geospatial auxiliary data. However, judicious applications require attention to numerical hazards and monitoring of residuals to detect anomalies. Otherwise, results are not necessarily reliable, and unreliable results can persist undetected. These hazards are not well recognized in the sample survey literature, which might explain the paucity of survey applications that use RRE, especially given the widespread applications of the closely related Kalman filter in engineering, econometrics, atmospheric sciences, and physical oceanography.

RRE is a powerful solution to difficult sample survey problems. It separates a large complex sample survey into smaller components, each of which is more easily addressed. These components are sequentially reassembled into more efficient and accurate population estimates. RRE offers the opportunity to consider complex sampling designs that would otherwise be too daunting.

Post-Stratification (PS) is a familiar and simple approach in large government survey programs of natural resources, such as FIA and LUCAS. It poses no extraordinary risks. However, PS is an impediment to statistical efficiency and achievement of FIA strategic goals for remote sensing. RRE is slightly more complex, but it can improve efficiency by assimilating larger quantities of remotely sensed auxiliary information. Results from either estimator can be represented as expansion values in a plot-level database. Either RRE or PS can be applied post hoc, without disrupting investments in previous field measurements.

A decision to convert from PS to RRE depends on the compromise among implementation costs, risks, efficiency, accuracy, and long-term cost savings. The decision can be reversible. If the costs of implementation and risk management with RRE are unacceptable in a large government survey program, then RRE might remain an attractive choice for special analytical studies whenever extra accuracy merits extra effort.

Acknowledgments

Javier Gallego, Lorenzo Fattorini, KaDonna Randolph, David Turner, and three anonymous reviewers contributed valuable comments and suggestions that significantly improved earlier drafts. Any remaining errors or omissions are my sole responsibility.

Endnotes

[1] FIA uses an infinite-population model of points, each with a 0.067-ha support region (Reams and others 2005a). The FIA sampling frame is approximately a 5-km systematic triangular grid (Bechtold and Scott 2005). The total sample size in the USA is approximately 360,000 Primary Sampling Units (PSUs), of which 30 percent sample forest conditions.

[2] In 2001, LUCAS used a systematic sample of 90-ha cluster plots (PSUs) on an 18-km systematic rectangular grid, with a total sample size of approximately 10,000 PSUs.

[3] The EU15 are those nations in the European Union prior to May 2004: Austria, Belgium, Denmark, Finland, France, Germany, Greece, Ireland, Italy, Luxembourg, the Netherlands, Portugal, Spain, Sweden, and the United Kingdom.

[4] The census of full-coverage remotely sensed pixels may be composed of images acquired at different dates, which are subsequently merged into a single multivariate database containing all pixels in the population. Even so, some portions of the population may be obscured by clouds, cloud shadows, haze, or missing pixel measurements. Obscured pixels may be treated as a category separate from the CORINE categories land cover. To reduce complexity, the obscured condition is not illustrated in the CORINE example.

[5] Särndal and others (1992) use the term "study-variables" for the target statistics, such as area of forest. Zhang (2000) uses the equivalent term "object-variables," and Rao (2003) uses the term "variables of interest."

[6] See Maybeck (1979) and Czaplewski (2010) for the more general case in which the random measurement errors are not independent of the random estimation errors for the state-vector.

[7] Gallego and Bamps (2008) did not report exact sample size. The approximation of $m = 1114$ is merely an example.

[8] Gallego and Bamps (2008) use 17 categories that are simplifications of the 44 CORINE categories. These are further collapsed here into 12 categories as a more concise example.

[9] Gallego and Bamps (2008) use 12 categories that are simplifications of the 57 LUCAS categories for land cover and 14 categories of land use. These are further collapsed here into nine categories as a more concise example.

[10] The multivariate census of pixel values in Equation 1 has the null covariance matrix $R = 0$. Therefore, it is not exactly analogous to the univariate composite estimator.

[11] All computations and data storage should use double precision numerics to reduce insidious round-off errors.

[12] Figure 2 displays the standardized residuals with the normal distribution as a backdrop. The purpose is to emphasize that two residuals have unexpectedly extreme values. The expectation of zero mean and unit variance is a necessary component of the proposed analysis of residuals. However, the choice of the normal distribution is merely an assumption, which cannot be rigorously tested with 12 residuals.

[13] Czaplewski (2001) makes a similar connection through the perspective of the matrix inversion lemma as applied by Householder (1964).

[14] The margins of the contingency table are sufficient statistics to estimate the sample covariance matrix for a multinomial variable (e.g., Fattorini and others 2004).

References

Agresti, A. 2007. An introduction to categorical data analysis. Wiley series in probability and statistics. John Wiley & Sons, Inc.: Hoboken, NJ. 2nd edition. 400 p.

Bar-Shalom, Y., X.-R. Li, and T. Kirubarajan. 2001. Estimation with applications to tracking and navigation. John Wiley & Sons, Inc.: New York. 584 p.

Bauer, M.E., M.M. Hixson, and B.J. Davis. 1978. Area estimation of crops by digital analysis of Landsat data. Photogrammetric Engineering and Remote Sensing 44(8):1033-1043.

Bechtold, W.A., and P.L. Patterson, eds. 2005. The enhanced Forest Inventory and Analysis program—national sampling design and estimation procedures. USDA For. Serv. Gen. Tech. Rep. SRS-80. 85 p.

Bechtold, W.A., and C.T. Scott. 2005. The Forest Inventory and Analysis plot design, P. 27-42 in: The enhanced Forest Inventory and Analysis program—national sampling design and estimation procedures, W.A. Bechtold and P.L. Patterson, eds. USDA For. Serv. Gen. Tech. Rep. SRS-80.

Bickford, A., C. Mayer, and K. Ware. 1963. An efficient sampling design for forest inventory: the northeastern forest resurvey. Journal of Forestry 61:826-833.

Bierman, G.J. 1977. Factorization methods for discrete sequential estimation, vol. 123 of Mathematics in science and engineering. Academic Press: New York. 241 p.

Binder, D.A., and M.A. Hidiroglou. 1988. Sampling in time. P. 187-211 in: Handbook of statistics: sampling, vol. 6, chapt. 8, P.R. Krishnaiah, and C.R. Rao, eds. Elsevier.

Blackard, J.A., M.V. Finco, E.H. Helmer, G.R. Holden, M.L. Hoppus, D.M. Jacobs, A.J. Lister, G.G. Moisen, M.D. Nelson, R. Riemann, B. Ruefenacht, D. Salajanu, D.L. Weyermann, K.C. Winterberger, T.J. Brandeis, R.L. Czaplewski, R.E. McRoberts, P.L. Patterson, and R.P. Tymcio. 2008. Mapping U.S. forest biomass using nationwide forest inventory data and moderate resolution information. Remote Sensing of Environment 112:1658-1677.

Bound, J., C. Brown, and N. Mathiowetz. 2001. Measurement error in survey data. P. 3705-3843 in: Handbook of econometrics, vol. 5, chapt. 59, J.J. Heckman and E. Leamer, eds. Elsevier.

Breidt, J., and J. Opsomer. 2008. Endogenous post-stratification in surveys: classifying with a sample-fitted model. Annals of Statistics 36:403-427.

Carfagna, E., and J.F. Gallego, 2005. Using remote sensing for agricultural statistics. International Statistical Review 73(3):389-404.

Carlson, T.N., and D.A. Ripley. 1997. On the relation between NDVI, fractional vegetation cover, and leaf area index. Remote Sensing of Environment 62:241-252.

Chui, C.K., and G. Chen 2009. Kalman filtering with real-time applications. Springer series in information sciences, vol. 17. 4th ed. 229 p.

Cochran, W.G. 1977. Sampling techniques. John Wiley & Sons: New York. 3rd ed. 448 p.

Congalton, R. 1991. A review of assessing the accuracy of classifications of remotely sensed data. Remote Sensing of Environment 37(1):35-46.

Coulston, J. 2008. Forest inventory and stratified estimation: a cautionary note. USDA For. Serv. Res. Note SRS-16. 8 p.

Czaplewski, R. 2001. Areal control using generalized least squares as an alternative to stratification. P. 63-65 in: Proceedings of the second annual Forest Inventory and Analysis symposium, G.A. Reams, R.E. McRoberts, and P.C. Van Deusen, eds. USDA For. Serv. Gen. Tech. Rep. SRS-47.

Czaplewski, R.L. 1992. Misclassification bias in areal estimates. Photogrammetric Engineering and Remote Sensing 58:189-192.

Czaplewski, R.L. 1994. Variance approximations for assessments of classification accuracy. USDA For. Serv. Res. Pap. RM-316. 29 p.

Czaplewski, R.L. 1999. Multistage remote sensing: toward an annual national inventory. Journal of Forestry 97:44-48.

Czaplewski, R.L. 2005. Re-sampling remotely sensed data to improve national and regional mapping of forest conditions with confidential field data. P. 262-284 in: Workshop proceedings: quantitative techniques for deriving national-scale data, M. Marsden, M. Downing, and M. Riffe, eds.

Czaplewski, R.L. 2010. Complex sample survey estimation in static state-space. USDA For. Serv. Gen. Tech. Rep. RMRS-GTR-239. Fort Collins, CO.

Czaplewski, R.L., and P.L. Patterson. 2001. Accuracy of remotely sensed classifications for stratification of forest and non-forest lands. P. 32-42 in: Proceedings of the second annual Forest Inventory and Analysis symposium, G.A. Reams, R.E. McRoberts, and P.C. Van Deusen, eds. USDA For. Serv. Gen. Tech. Rep. SRS-47.

Czaplewski, R.L., and P.L. Patterson. 2003. Classification accuracy for stratification with remotely sensed data. Forest Science 49:402-408.

de Gruijter, J., D. Brus, M. Bierkens, and M. Knotters. 2006. Sampling for natural resource monitoring. Springer-Verlag: Berlin, Heidelberg. 332 p.

Deville, J.C., and C.E. Särndal. 1992. Calibration estimators in survey sampling. Journal of the American Statistical Association 87:376-382.

Deville, J.C., C.E. Särndal, and O. Sautory. 1993. Generalized raking procedures in survey sampling. Journal of the American Statistical Association 88:1013-1020.

Diderrich, G.T. 1985. The Kalman filter from the perspective of Goldberger-Theil estimators. The American Statistician 39:193-198.

Doran, H. 1997. Applying linear time-varying constraints to econometric models: with an application to demand systems. Journal of Economics 79:83-95.

Dryver, A.L. 1999. Adaptive sampling designs and associated estimators. State College, PA: Pennsylvania State University, Department of Statistics. 127 p. Dissertation. Available: http://as.nida.ac.th/~dryver/dissertation.pdf.

Duncan, D.B., and S.D. Horn. 1972. Linear dynamic recursive estimation from the viewpoint of regression analysis. Journal of the American Statistical Association 67:815-821.

Estevao, V.M., and C-E. Särndal. 2004. Borrowing strength is not the best technique within a wide class of design-consistent domain estimators. Journal of Official Statistics 20:645-669.

Estevao, V.M., and C-E. Särndal. 2006. Survey estimates by calibration on complex auxiliary information. International Statistical Review 74:127-147.

Fattorini, L., M. Marcheselli, and C. Pisani. 2004. Two-phase estimation of coverages with second-phase corrections. Environmetrics 15:357-368.

Frescino, T.S., G.G. Moisen, K.A. Megown, V.J. Nelson, E.A. Freeman, P.L. Patterson, M. Finco, K. Brewer, and J. Menlove. 2009. Nevada Photo-Based Inventory Pilot (NPIP) photo sampling procedures. USDA For. Serv. Gen. Tech. Rep. RMRS-GTR-222. 30 p.

Gallego, F.J. 2004. Remote sensing and land cover area estimation. International Journal of Remote Sensing 25:3019-3047.

Gallego, F.J., and J. Delincé. 2010. The European Land Use and Cover Area-frame Survey (LUCAS) P. 151-166 in: Agricultural survey methods. R. Benedetti, M. Bee, G. Espa, F. Piersimoni, eds. John Wiley and Sons, Inc. 434 p.

Gallego, J., and C. Bamps. 2008. Using CORINE land cover and the point survey LUCAS for area estimation. International Journal of Applied Earth Observation and Geoinformation 10:467-475.

Gregoire, T.G., and D.K. Walters. 1988. Composite vector estimators derived by weighting inversely proportional to variance. Canadian Journal of Forest Research 18:282-284.

Grewal, M.S., and A.P. Andrews. 2001. Kalman filtering: theory and practice using MATLAB. John Wiley & Sons, Inc.: Hoboken, NJ. 592 p.

Hahn, J.T., C.D. MacClean, S.L. Arner, and W.A. Bechtold. 1995. Procedures to handle inventory cluster plots that straddle two or more conditions. Forest Science Monograph 31:12-25.

Halme, M., and E. Tomppo. 2001. Improving the accuracy of multisource forest inventory estimates to reducing plot location error—a multicriteria approach. Remote Sensing of Environment 78:321-327.

Hay, A.M. 1988. The derivation of global estimates from a confusion matrix. International Journal of Remote Sensing 9:1395-1398.

Healey, S., W. Cohen, Y. Zhiqiang, and O. Krankina. 2005. Comparison of tasseled cap-based Landsat data structures for use in forest disturbance detection. Remote Sensing of Environment 97:301-310.

Heinl, M., J. Walde, G. Tappeiner, and U. Tappeiner. 2009. Classifiers vs. input variables—the drivers in image classification for land cover mapping. International Journal of Applied Earth Observation and Geoinformation 11:423-430.

Householder, A. 1964. The theory of matrices in numerical analysis. Dover Publications. 257 p.

Houston, A.G., and F.G. Hall. 1984. Use of satellite data in agricultural surveys. Communications in Statistics—Theory and Methods 13:2857-2880.

Jagers, P. 1986. Post-stratification against bias in sampling. International Statistical Review 54:159-167.

Jazwinski, A.H. 1970. Stochastic processes and filtering. Academic Press: New York. 376 p.

Kalman, R.E., P.L. Falb, and M.A. Arbib. 1969. Topics in mathematical system theory. International series in pure and applied mathematics. McGraw-Hill: New York. 358 p.

Katila, M., and E. Tomppo. 2001. Selecting estimation parameters for the Finnish multisource national forest inventory. Remote Sensing of Environment 76:16-32.

King, R.B. 2002. Land cover mapping principles: a return to interpretation fundamentals. International Journal of Remote Sensing 23(18):3525-3545.

Kleeschulte, S., and G. Büttner. 2006. European land cover mapping: the CORINE experience. P. 31-44 in: North American land cover summit, AAG special issue, chapt. 4. J.H. Smith, ed. Association of American Geographers: Washington, DC.

Knottnerus, P. 2003. Sample survey theory: some Pythagorean perspectives. Springer-Verlag: New York. 415 p.

Ledoit, O., and M. Wolf. 2004. A well-conditioned estimator for large-dimensional covariance matrices. Journal of Multivariate Analysis 88:365-411.

Magnussen, S. 2003. Stepwise estimators for three-phase sampling of categorical variables. Journal of Applied Statistics 30(5):461-475.

Mandallaz, D. 2008. Sampling techniques for forest inventories. Chapman & Hall: New York. 256 p.

Mas, J.F., and J.J. Flores. 2008. The application of artificial neural networks to the analysis of remotely sensed data. International Journal of Remote Sensing 29:617-663.

Matérn, B. 1960. Spatial variation: stochastic models and their applications to some problems in forest surveys and other sampling investigations. Meddelanden från Statens Skogsforskningsinstitut 49:1-144.

Maybeck, P.S. 1979. Stochastic models, estimation, and control, volume 141-1 of Mathematics in science and engineering. Academic Press: New York. 423 p.

McRoberts, R., W. Bechtold, P. Patterson, C. Scott, and G. Reams. 2005a. The enhanced Forest Inventory and Analysis program of the USDA Forest Service: historical perspective and announcements of statistical documentation. Journal of Forestry 103:304-308.

McRoberts, R.E., G.R. Holden, M.D. Nelson, G.C. Liknes, and D.D. Gormanson. 2005b. Using satellite imagery as ancillary data for increasing the precision of estimates for the Forest Inventory and Analysis program of the USDA Forest Service. Canadian Journal of Forest Research 35:2968-2980.

McRoberts, R.E., D.G. Wendt, M.D. Nelson, and M.H. Hansen. 2002. Using a land cover classification based on satellite imagery to improve the precision of forest inventory area estimates. Remote Sensing of Environment 81:36-44.

McRoberts, R.E. 1999. Joint annual forest inventory and monitoring system: the North Central perspective. Journal of Forestry 97:27-31.

McRoberts, R.E. 2005. The enhanced Forest Inventory and Analysis program. P. 1-10 in: The enhanced Forest Inventory and Analysis program—national sampling design and estimation procedures, W.A. Bechtold and P.L. Patterson, eds. USDA For. Serv. Gen. Tech. Rep. SRS-80.

McRoberts, R.E. 2006. A model-based approach to inventory stratification. P. 87-91 in: Proceedings of the sixth annual Forest Inventory and Analysis symposium; 2004 September 21-24; Denver, CO; R.E. McRoberts, G.A. Reams, P.C. Van Deusen, W.H. McWilliams, eds. USDA For. Serv. Gen. Tech. Rep. WO-70. 126 p.

Nelson, M., G. Moisen, M. Finco, and K. Brewer. 2007. Forest Inventory and Analysis in the United States: remote sensing and geospatial activities. Photogrammetric Engineering and Remote Sensing 73:729-732.

Nelson, M.D., R.E. McRoberts, G.R. Holden, and M.E. Bauer. 2009. Effects of satellite image spatial aggregation and resolution on estimates of forest land area. International Journal of Remote Sensing 30(8):1913-1940.

Patterson, P.L., and G.A. Reams. 2005. Combining panels for forest inventory and analysis estimation. P. 79-84 in: The enhanced forest inventory and analysis program—national sampling design and estimation procedures, P.L. Patterson, and G.A. Reams, eds. USDA For. Serv. Gen. Tech. Rep. SRS-80.

Purcell, N.J., and L. Kish. 1979. A biometrics invited paper. Estimation for small domains. Biometrics 35:365-384.

Rao, J.N.K. 2003. Small area estimation. John Wiley and Sons, Inc.: Hoboken, NJ. 313 p.

Reams, G., B. Smith, B. Bechtold, R. McRoberts, F. Spirek, and C. Liff. 2005a. Three proposed data collection models for annual inventories. USDA For. Serv. Gen. Tech. Rep. WO-69. 222 p.

Reams, G.A., W.D. Smith, M.H. Hansen, W.A. Bechtold, F.A. Roesch, and G.G. Moisen. 2005b. The Forest Inventory and Analysis sampling frame. P. 31-36 in: The enhanced forest inventory and analysis program—national sampling design and estimation procedures, P.L. Patterson, and G.A. Reams, eds. USDA For. Serv. Gen. Tech. Rep. SRS-80.

Sader, S., M. Hoppus, J. Metzler, and S. Jin. 2005. Perspectives of Maine forest cover change from Landsat imagery and Forest Inventory Analysis (FIA). Journal of Forestry 103:299-303.

Särndal, C-E., B. Swensson, J.H. Wretman. 1992. Model assisted survey sampling. Springer-Verlag: New York. 694 p.

Schowengerdt, R.A. 2007. Remote sensing: models and methods for image processing. Elsevier. 3rd ed. 560 p.

Scott, C.T., W.A. Bechtold, G.A. Reams, W.D. Smith, J.A. Westfall, M.H., Hansen, and G.G. Moisen. 2005. Sample-based estimators used by the Forest Inventory and Analysis national information management system. P. 53-77 in: The enhanced forest inventory and analysis program—national sampling design and estimation procedures, P.L. Patterson, and G.A. Reams, eds. USDA For. Serv. Gen. Tech. Rep. SRS-80.

Simon, D., and T.L. Chia. 2002. Kalman filtering with state equality constraints. IEEE Aerospace and Electronic Systems 38(1):128-136.

Smith, W.B. 2002. Forest Inventory and Analysis: a national inventory and monitoring program. Environmental Pollution 116:S233-S242.

Sõstra, K., and I. Traat. 2009. Optimal domain estimation under summation restriction. Journal of Statistical Planning and Inference 139:3928-3941.

Stehman, S.V., and R.L. Czaplewski. 1998. Design and analysis for thematic map accuracy assessment: fundamental principles. Remote Sensing of Environment 64:331-344.

Theil, H., and A.S. Goldberger. 1961. On pure and mixed statistical estimation in economics. International Review of Economics 2:65-78.

Tomppo, E. 2002. Simultaneous use of Landsat-TM and IRS-1C WiFS data in estimating large area tree stem volume and aboveground biomass. Remote Sensing of Environment 82:156-171.

Tomppo, E., and M. Halme. 2004. Using coarse scale forest variables as ancillary information and weighting of variables in k-NN estimation: a genetic algorithm approach. Remote Sensing of Environment 92:1-20.

Van Deusen, P.C. 2005. Stratified forest inventory estimation with mapped plots. Canadian Journal of Forest Research 35:2382-2386.

Verbeke, G., and G. Molenberghs. 2000. Linear mixed models for longitudinal data. Springer: New York. 568 p.

Vogelmann, J.E., T. Sohl, and S.M. Howard. 1998. Regional characterization of land cover using multiple sources of data. Photogrammetric Engineering and Remote Sensing 64:45-58.

Wolter, K.M. 1979. Composite estimation in finite populations. Journal of the American Statistical Association 74(367):604-613.

Zhang, L. 2000. Post-stratification and calibration—a synthesis. Journal of the American Statistical Association 54:178-184.

Appendix A: Approximate Sample Covariance Matrices

Gallego and Bamps (2008) do not provide sufficient statistics to reproduce their covariance matrices. This covariance matrix is needed for Equation 3 and to compare efficiency of RRE with Gallego and Bamps' Post-Stratification (PS) estimate. The following approximation is based on the multinomial distribution, which assumes simple random sampling of $n = 1114$ homogeneous PSUs[7]. In reality, each PSU is a heterogeneous cluster plot, which is expected to be more efficient. Therefore, the approximation for Equation 3 is heuristically scaled using relative efficiencies reported by Gallego and Bamps in their Table 4. Additional assumptions about relative sampling errors for the CORINE variables were employed to assure that the residuals do not exceed four standard deviation units.

The approximation begins with the multinomial second moment matrix

$$\hat{\mathbf{V}}\left(\hat{\mathbf{t}}_{\text{LUCAS}}\right)_{\text{MULTNOMIAL}} = \frac{361800^2}{1114}\left(\text{diag}\left(\hat{\mathbf{t}}_{\text{LUCAS}}\right) - \hat{\mathbf{t}}_{\text{LUCAS}}\hat{\mathbf{t}}'_{\text{LUCAS}}\right) \tag{25}$$

where $A = 361,800$-ha. See Knottnerus (2003 p. 367) or Fattorini and others (2004) for details on the covariance matrix for a vector representation of a multinomial variable.

The covariance matrix for systematic sampling is approximated with the 108-by-108 diagonal scaling matrix $\mathbf{H}_{\text{SYS}}$ to estimate the covariance matrix needed in Equation 3:

$$\hat{\mathbf{V}}\left(\hat{\mathbf{t}}_{\text{LUCAS}}\right)_{\text{SYS}} = \mathbf{H}_{\text{SYS}}\left[\hat{\mathbf{V}}\left(\hat{\mathbf{t}}_{\text{LUCAS}}\right)_{\text{MULTNOMIAL}}\right]\mathbf{H}_{\text{SYS}}, \text{ where } \mathbf{H}_{\text{SYS}} = \text{diag}\begin{bmatrix} 1 \\ 1 \\ 1 \\ 70 \\ 1 \\ 1 \\ 5 \\ 1 \\ 10 \\ 20 \\ 1 \\ 0.1 \end{bmatrix} \otimes \text{diag}\begin{bmatrix} 0.4605 \\ 0.5992 \\ 0.4950 \\ 0.4123 \\ 0.7358 \\ 0.9289 \\ 0.6378 \\ 0.9849 \\ 0.8852 \end{bmatrix} \tag{26}$$

The covariance matrix for PS of the same sampling units with four strata, which is the improvement offered by Gallego and Bamps, is approximated with the 108-by-108 diagonal scaling matrix $\mathbf{H}_{\text{STR}}$:

$$\hat{\mathbf{V}}\left(\hat{\mathbf{t}}_{\text{LUCAS}}\right)_{\text{STR}} = \mathbf{H}_{\text{STR}}\left[\hat{\mathbf{V}}\left(\hat{\mathbf{t}}_{\text{LUCAS}}\right)_{\text{MULTNOMIAL}}\right]\mathbf{H}_{\text{STR}}, \text{ where } \mathbf{H}_{\text{STR}} = \text{diag}\begin{bmatrix} 1 \\ 1 \\ 1 \\ 70 \\ 1 \\ 1 \\ 5 \\ 1 \\ 10 \\ 20 \\ 1 \\ 0.1 \end{bmatrix} \otimes \text{diag}\begin{bmatrix} 0.3725 \\ 0.4932 \\ 0.4424 \\ 0.3823 \\ 0.6311 \\ 0.8413 \\ 0.5634 \\ 0.8955 \\ 0.8394 \end{bmatrix} \tag{27}$$

where the "diag" operator creates a diagonal matrix with the object vector placed on the matrix diagonal. With these approximations, PS reduces the trace of the covariance matrix in Equation 27 by 0.80 times the trace of the covariance matrix with systematic sampling alone (Equation 26), which, in turn, is about 0.50 times the trace of the covariance matrix, assuming homogeneous PSUs rather than heterogeneous cluster plots (Equation 25).

Appendix B: Simplification with Multinomial Distribution

This Appendix briefly considers reduction in the dimensions of RRE. It uses the margins of the contingency table instead of the entire table. In the example given in Table 1, there are 12 CORINE categories in the auxiliary census statistics and 9 categories in the target LUCAS-2001 classification system. Equations 2 to 24 use the $(12 \times 9 = 108)$-by-1 vector estimate of this 12-by-9 contingency table. This posed no detectable numerical problems with RRE. However, constraints on categorical auxiliary census variables might further enlarge the dimensions, which can accumulate numerical errors.

Dimensions may be reduced to a $(12 + 9 = 21)$-by-1 vector using the margins of the contingency table rather than all interior cells of Table 1. If the individual cell estimates are of no particular interest, then attention focuses on optimal estimation of the 9-by-1 vector of LUCAS-2001 variables on the column margin of Table 1. From Equations 15 and 22

$$\left(\hat{\mathbf{t}}_{\text{RRE}} \right)_y = \mathbf{H}_y \left(\hat{\mathbf{t}}_{\text{RRE}} \right)$$

$$= \mathbf{H}_y \hat{\mathbf{t}}_{yx} + \mathbf{H}_y \mathbf{K} \left(\mathbf{t}_x - \hat{\mathbf{t}}_x \right) \tag{28}$$

where $\left(\hat{\mathbf{t}}_{\text{RRE}} \right)$ is 108-by-1, $\left(\hat{\mathbf{t}}_{\text{RRE}} \right)_y$ is 9-by-1, and $\left(\mathbf{t}_x - \hat{\mathbf{t}}_x \right)$ is 12-by-1. The 9-by-12 weighting matrix $\mathbf{H}_y \mathbf{K}$ in Equation 28 expands to

$$\mathbf{H}_y \mathbf{K} = \mathbf{H}_y \hat{\mathbf{V}} \left(\hat{\mathbf{t}}_{yx} \right) \mathbf{H}_x' \left[\mathbf{H}_x \hat{\mathbf{V}} \left(\hat{\mathbf{t}}_{yx} \right) \mathbf{H}_x' \right]^{-1}$$

$$= \hat{\mathbf{V}} \left(\hat{\mathbf{t}}_y \hat{\mathbf{t}}_x \right) \hat{\mathbf{V}} \left(\hat{\mathbf{t}}_x \right)^{-1} \tag{29}$$

where the 9-by-12 matrix $\hat{\mathbf{V}} \left(\hat{\mathbf{t}}_y \hat{\mathbf{t}}_x \right) = \mathbf{H}_y \hat{\mathbf{V}} \left(\hat{\mathbf{t}}_{yx} \right) \mathbf{H}_x'$ contains the estimated covariances among the row and column margins. In the special case of homogeneous point plots as the PSU, the multinomial distribution applies, and Equation 29 equals

$$\mathbf{H}_y \mathbf{K} = \left(\frac{-\hat{\mathbf{t}}_y \hat{\mathbf{t}}_x'}{m} \right) \left(\frac{\text{diag} \left(\hat{\mathbf{t}}_x \right) - \hat{\mathbf{t}}_x \hat{\mathbf{t}}_x'}{m} \right)^{-1} \tag{30}$$

Therefore, in this special case, the 12-by-1 row margin $\hat{\mathbf{t}}_x$ and the 9-by-1 column margin $\hat{\mathbf{t}}_y$ of Table 1 are sufficient statistics for RRE, and there is no loss of optimality when the cross-classified cell values are ignored. The same holds for Equation 26, where the 108-by-108 covariance matrix $\hat{\mathbf{V}} \left(\hat{\mathbf{t}}_{yx} \right) = \mathbf{H}_{\text{SYS}} \left[\left(\text{diag} \left(\hat{\mathbf{t}}_{yx} \right) - \hat{\mathbf{t}}_{yx}' \hat{\mathbf{t}}_{yx} \right) / m \right] \mathbf{H}_{\text{SYS}}'$.

In other cases, such as the LUCAS cluster plot, Equation 29 does not equal Equation 30, and sole use of the margins would yield a sub-optimal RRE. However, the 9-by-12 matrix difference $\left(\mathbf{H}_y \hat{\mathbf{V}} \left(\hat{\mathbf{t}}_{yx} \right) \mathbf{H}_x' \right) - \left(\hat{\mathbf{t}}_y \hat{\mathbf{t}}_x' \right) / m$

and the 12-by-12 matrix difference $\mathbf{H}_x\hat{\mathbf{V}}(\hat{\mathbf{t}}_{yx})\mathbf{H}_x' - (\text{diag}(\hat{\mathbf{t}}_x) - \hat{\mathbf{t}}_x\hat{\mathbf{t}}_x')/m$ can be relatively small and the sacrifice in optimality can be relatively minor. Estimates are readily made with both the 108-by-1 and 21-by-1 versions of the population-vector, and the differences between the resulting variance estimates would help guide the decision between efficiency and dimension reduction.